THE 2011 GRIFFIN POETRY PRIZE ANTHOLOGY

A Selection of the Shortlist

Edited by Tim Lilburn

ANANSI

This edition published in 2011 by
House of Anansi Press Inc.
110 Spadina Avenue, Suite 801
Toronto, ON, M5V 2K4
Tel. 416-363-4343
Fax 416-363-1017
www.anansi.ca

Distributed in Canada by
HarperCollins Canada Ltd.
1995 Markham Road
Scarborough, ON, M1B 5M8
Toll free tel. 1-800-387-0117

Distributed in the United States by
Publishers Group West
1700 Fourth Street
Berkeley, CA 94710
Toll free tel. 1-800-788-3123

House of Anansi Press is committed to protecting our natural environment. As part of our efforts, this book is printed on paper that contains 100% post-consumer recycled fibres, is acid-free, and is processed chlorine-free.

15 14 13 12 11   1 2 3 4 5

Library and Archives Canada Cataloguing in Publication

Cataloguing data available from Library and Archives Canada

Library of Congress Control Number: 2011926905

Cover design: Chloe Griffin and Kyra Griffin
Cover and interior images: Chloe Griffin
Typesetting: Sari Naworynski

Canada Council   Conseil des Arts
for the Arts   du Canada

ONTARIO ARTS COUNCIL
CONSEIL DES ARTS DE L'ONTARIO

We acknowledge for their financial support of our publishing program the Canada Council for the Arts, the Ontario Arts Council, and the Government of Canada through the Canada Book Fund.

Printed and bound in Canada

*Poetry in all its tongues
is to the initiate but a single language,
the language which sounded in Paradise
before it strayed into the wilderness.*

— Friedrich Rückert

CONTENTS

CANADIAN FINALISTS

PREFACE

The large boxes would come in batches of three or five, and I'd slice through the tape, lift their lids and smell the books inside. What a feast it was reading the hundreds of volumes of poetry. And, yes, there was something insane about it all: I'd have to take breaks of days to recover an unpoemed equilibrium. Restored, I'd be back in the pine rocker, under the wonky floor lamp, in the basement, absorbed. It was a delight to open each book and think — what next? What new form of risk and achievement am I going to witness now? There were dozens of writers, extraordinarily skilled practitioners, I'd never heard of and new work from people I'd been tracking for years.

Poetry is a kind of *lectio divina* of the age, a reading of landscapes, preoccupations, events, characters, that is supple enough, sufficiently permeable, to be stopped in its tracks. Its availability makes it capable of a kind of acute phenomenology of spirit. So where is poetry headed these days? There is no formal or thematic limit to the range of contemporary poetry, but in 2010 certain gestures kept re-appearing. Grief was one — for a parent with Alzheimer's, for an inability to conceive, for injustice exercised by the state against its citizens and men against women, for nature, for a destruction of sense; there were numerous meditations on 9/11. Some poets were preoccupied by retrieval — of the thought experiments of Archimedes, the ruminations of Marx, the bus routes of post-war Northern Ireland — and the use of what was saved and brought back as a device to comprehend the present. There was the appeal of unadorned looking: at snow, the view from Blomidon Mountain.

It was difficult choosing seven books that stood out, but during the long and enjoyable conference calls Colm Tóibín, Chase Twichell and I had this past March, we found ourselves returning repeatedly to the titles that eventually made up our shortlists. Gjertrud Schnackenberg's *Heavenly Questions* commanded our attention with its power of intelligence and deep sadness and Seamus Heaney's *Human Chain* with its precision, ingenuity, and emotional grab. Adonis claimed us with his gorgeous metaphorical leaps and the breadth of his political vision, while François Jacqmin persuaded us through his lack of ease in the writing of poetry itself.

The Canadian finalists were just as difficult to select but in the end the audacious reach of Dionne Brand's *Ossuaries*, the conviviality of John Steffler's *Lookout*, and the humour and courage of Suzanne Buffam's *The Irrationalist* won us over. Each of these quite different books had somehow managed, rather magnificently, to complete the tasks that their respective voices had set them. Their languages burned with specificity, as their authors worked through terrains of radical thought, the barrens of Newfoundland and contemporary unreason, with beauty and care in naming.

It was moving to see so many poets devoting what seemed to be the whole energy of their lives to a pastime that most people, in the Western world at least, greet with indifference. Poetry's lack of importance, however, is an illusion. Even when poets aren't putting conscious effort into addressing the society in which their work is written, that work is still an agent of transformation; something in the structure of poetry itself makes it so. Khaled Mattawa, in his introduction to Adonis's *Selected Poems*, quotes the Syrian poet on the difference between classical poetry with its commitment to the transmission of "clear and ready-made thoughts" and the new poetry emerging over the last few decades in Arabic culture, where the poet "sets his words as traps or nets to catch an unknown world." Sitting in the pine rocker last winter, I saw world after world netted in ingenious language. Mattawa notes that Adonis "argues that a revolution in the arts and in how they are received can generate imaginative strategies at all levels of society." Reading the 2010 Griffin submissions, I found myself convinced again by poetry's visionary and subversive power.

Tim Lilburn, March 2011

INTERNATIONAL
FINALISTS

KHALED MATTAWA (translator)

ADONIS

Selected Poems

Adonis, along with Saadi Yousef and Mahmoud Darwish, has helped to bring into being modern Arabic poetry. Masterfully translated by Khaled Mattawa, his *Selected Poems* show a range comparable to Lorca's, stretching from the sensuous to the political. When he left the Syrian socialist party in the early Sixties, Adonis left all traditional politics behind only to become committed to deep cultural transformation through the creative energies of poetry, in a quest for what could be called an Arabic modernism. In the case of his poetry, this new mode takes the form of a combination of metaphysics, interiority and solidarity, a hybrid present as well in the poetry of Rumi and the thought of Ibn Arabi. "I sang of gardens and a towering palace / while in wretchedness, in attics hid. / Tell him who used to sleep on soft cushions / that the heights are being punished by a star." From the swooping, Whitman-esque, epic voice of the early *Songs of Mihyar of Damascus*, to the erotic mysticism of the long poem "Body" and the subdued meditations of *Beginnings of the Body, Ends of the Sea*, we are in the presence of a poet of global importance.

Psalm

He comes bereft like a forest and like clouds, irrefutable. Yesterday he carried a continent and moved the sea from its place.

He draws the unseen side of day, kindles daylight in his footsteps, borrows the shoes of night and waits for what never comes. He is the physics of things. He knows them and gives them names he never reveals. He is reality and its opposite, life and its other.

When stone becomes a lake and shadow a city, he comes alive, alive and eludes despair, erasing a clearing for hope to dwell, and dancing so the dirt will yawn, and trees fall asleep.

Here he is announcing the lines of peripheries, etching a sign of magic on the brow of our age.

He fills life and no one sees him. He shapes life into foam and dives. He turns tomorrow into prey and chases desperately after it. His words are chiseled on the compass of loss, loss, loss.

Bewilderment is his country, though he is studded with eyes.
He terrorizes and rejuvenates.
He drips shock and overflows with ridicule.
He peels the human being like an onion.

He is the wind that never retreats, water that never returns to its source. He creates a race that begins with him. He has no offspring, no roots to his steps.
He walks the abyss, tall as the wind.

Not a Star

Not a star, not a prophet's inspiration
not a pious face worshipping the moon,
here he comes like a pagan spear
invading the land of alphabets
bleeding, raising his hemorrhage to the sun.
Here he comes wearing the stone's nakedness
thrusting his prayers into caves.

Here he comes
embracing the weightless earth.

Flower of Alchemy

I must travel to a paradise of ashes,
walk among its hidden trees.
In ash, myths, diamonds, and golden fleece.

I must travel through hunger, through roses, toward harvest.
I must travel, must rest
under the bow of orphaned lips.

On orphaned lips, in their wounded shade
the flower of that old alchemy.

Man's Song

Sideways,
I glimpsed your face drawn on the trunk of a palm
and saw the sun, black in your hands.
I tied my longing to that tree and carried night in a basket
                                    carried the whole city
and scattered myself before your eyes.
                        Then I saw your face hungry like a child's.
I circled it with invocations
and above it I sprinkled jasmine buds.

Woman's Song

Sideways,
I caught sight of his old man's face
robbed by days and sorrows.
He came to me holding his green jars to his chest
rushing to the last supper.
Each jar was a bay
and a wedding held for a harbor and a boat
where days and shores drown
where seagulls probe their past and sailors divine the future.
He came to me hungry and I stretched my love toward him,
a loaf of bread, a glass cup, and a bed.
I opened the doors to wind and sun
and shared with him the last supper.

I Imagine a Poet

A salute to Jacques Berque

I imagine a poet
in Beirut, sister to Anatolia, friend of Athens,
a poet who stands with his friend Jacques Berque at the gate of the sea
leaning on his cane.
I imagine his voice as the sound of a tambourine,
that the tambourine is broken in his throat,
that his throat is a fire named God.

I imagine a poet
into whose innards history pours
drenching his words and pooling at his feet,
a poet who rains blood that some hoist as a banner made of sky.

Goddess of doubt, you who were born in the lap of our mother the sea,
why do you not announce this poet and his friend?
Say what you do not see,
what turns time on its back,
what holds the wind standing on tiptoe,
what pours the ashes of silence on the flames of speech
improvised by the world's prose.
Announce also the inflamed eyelashes
the severed hands
the withered days

and whether the lantern is a throat or a head
and how we can distinguish today between an insect and a flower.
And say is there a means now
to colonize the clouds?
And say
how this Mediterranean still needs
to reemerge from the childhood of the alphabet.

Alphabet, how brave they are these cicadas that inhabit your harvest,
how ferocious these angels that lie in the beds of your forgetfulness!
René Char
where is the storm then,
and why is poetry still an ally of the waves
and why has the sky left nothing of our history
except statues whose genitals have been cut off?

The poet leaning on his cane
standing at the gate of the sea, with his friend
Jacques Berque
whispers to his friend, or perhaps to the waves:
"If there is a sky, it is migration."

And his friends replies, also whispering,
"No
the miracle is not above;
it's the soil sleeping among the underclothes of the grass."

What time is it now? I don't know
except that the spidery arms of the clock spin. Two or three flies circle and
    buzz above.
Poet, write a poem, and describe the scene
adding the wall upon which you were hung   and the curtain
half torn under the lamp   and the black window.
Do not forget to allude to modernity   so that you may be counted
among the pioneers, but before that, don't forget to describe the scene,
the old shoe resting alone   under the clock as if
waiting for its owner's return, and beware of the big issues: Poetry
must capture — not the things — but their crumbs.
And let your words rise to their covenant.

Owah!
The moon has fallen sad asleep
on his chair covered with clouds.
And the poet leaning on his cane accompanied
by his friend Jacques Berque
counted the moths that drowned in the clamor of the flame
on that night,
the flame of candles lit by children
who spend their nights standing in foam
hunting the waves.

An evening in Beirut,
lost and pining like a beggar soliciting in the vastness of space
brought down to his knees
resting his cheek on Ulysses' cheek.
Do we think we are still alive by the shore of the Mediterranean,

have we become herders of the stars?
A rose carries the whole of night in her sleeves,
leans on Beirut's chest,
and gives her waist to the air's forearm
while life embraces her hatchlings
placing her feet on the staircase of the future.

Is this really the world?
Shall I grieve? Shall I hope?
I prefer to sing.

SEAMUS HEANEY

Human Chain

The poems in Seamus Heaney's *Human Chain* contain tones and phrases that are perfectly tuned; they are true to memory and loss, and somehow miraculously they also manage to offer a vision of what is above or beyond the mere facts. The feeling is elegiac but also loosened and buoyant. Memory in these poems is filled with tones of regret and undertones of anguish, but it can also appear in cadences of hard-won wonder. There is an active urge in the rhythms of these poems to capture the living breath of things; sometimes the breath is hushed, and other times wise and resigned in its way of holding rhythms in and then releasing them. In the most ambitious poem, Heaney wanders in the shadow of Virgil's *Aeneid*, making his own journey in memory across Northern Ireland, allowing images and recollections in all their sonorous beauty to hit sharply against the sense of a time that has past, and can be recovered now in ways which are controlled but insistent in these poems.

Route 110

For Anna Rose

i

In a stained front-buttoned shopcoat —
Sere brown piped with crimson —
Out of the Classics bay into an aisle

Smelling of dry rot and disinfectant
She emerges, absorbed in her coin-count,
Eyes front, right hand at work

In the slack marsupial vent
Of her change-pocket, thinking what to charge
For a used copy of *Aeneid VI.*

Dustbreath bestirred in the cubicle mouth
I inhaled as she slid my purchase
Into a deckle-edged brown paper bag.

ii

Smithfield Market Saturdays. The pet shop
Fetid with droppings in the rabbit cages,
Melodious with canaries, green and gold,

But silent now as birdless Lake Avernus.
I hurried on, shortcutting to the buses,
Parrying the crush with my bagged Virgil,

Past booths and the jambs of booths with their displays
Of canvas schoolbags, maps, prints, plaster plaques,
Feather dusters, artificial flowers,

Then racks of suits and overcoats that swayed
When one was tugged from its overcrowded frame
Like their owners' shades close-packed on Charon's barge.

iii

Once the driver wound a little handle
The destination names began to roll
Fast-forward in their panel, and everything

Came to life. Passengers
Flocked to the kerb like agitated rooks
Around a rookery, all go

But undecided. At which point the inspector
Who ruled the roost in bus station and bus
Separated and directed everybody

By calling not the names but the route numbers,
And so we scattered as instructed, me
For Route 110, Cookstown via Toome and Magherafelt.

iv

Tarpaulin-stiff, coal-black, sharp-cuffed as slate,
The standard-issue railway guard's long coat
I bought once second-hand: suffering its scourge

At the neck and wrists was worth it even so
For the dismay I caused by doorstep night arrivals,
A creature of cold blasts and flap-winged rain.

And then, come finer weather, up and away
To Italy, in a wedding guest's bargain suit
Of finest weave, loose-fitting, summery, grey

As Venus' doves, hotfooting it with the tanned expats
Up their Etruscan slopes to a small brick chapel
To find myself the one there most at home.

v

Venus' doves? Why not McNicholls' pigeons
Out of their pigeon holes but homing still?
They lead unerringly to McNicholls' kitchen

And a votive jampot on the dresser shelf.
So reach me not a gentian but stalks
From the bunch that stood in it, each head of oats

A silvered smattering, each individual grain
Wrapped in a second husk of glittering foil
They'd saved from chocolate bars, then pinched and cinched

"To give the wee altar a bit of shine."
The night old Mrs. Nick, as she was to us,
Handed me one it as good as lit me home.

vi

It was the age of ghosts. Of hand-held flashlamps.
Lights moving at a distance scried for who
And why: whose wake, say, in which house on the road

In that direction — Michael Mulholland's the first
I attended as a full participant,
Sitting up until the family rose

Like strangers to themselves and us. A wake
Without the corpse of their own dear ill-advised
Sonbrother swimmer, lost in the Bristol Channel.

For three nights we kept conversation going
Around the waiting trestles. By the fourth
His coffin, with the lid on, was in place.

vii

The corpse house then a house of hospitalities
Right through the small hours, the ongoing card game
Interrupted constantly by rounds

Of cigarettes on plates, biscuits, cups of tea,
The antiphonal recital of known events
And others rare, clandestine, undertoned.

Apt pupil in their night school, I walked home
On the last morning, my clothes as smoke-imbued
As if I'd fed a pyre, accompanied to the gable

By the mother, to point out a right of way
Across their fields, into our own back lane,
And absolve me thus formally of trespass.

viii

As one when the month is young sees a new moon
Fading into daytime, again it is her face
At the dormer window, her hurt still new,

My look behind me hurried as I unlock,
Switch on, rev up, pull out and drive away
In the car she'll not have taken her eyes off,

The brakelights flicker-flushing at the corner
Like red lamps swung by RUC patrols
In the small hours on pre-Troubles roads

After dances, after our holdings on
And holdings back, the necking
And nay-saying age of impurity.

ix

And what in the end was there left to bury
Of Mr. Lavery, blown up in his own pub
As he bore the primed device and bears it still

Mid-morning towards the sun-admitting door
Of Ashley House? Or of Louis O'Neill
In the wrong place the Wednesday they buried

Thirteen who'd been shot in Derry? Or of bodies
Unglorified, accounted for and bagged
Behind the grief cordons: not to be laid

In war graves with full honours, nor in a separate plot
Fired over on anniversaries
By units drilled and spruce and unreconciled.

x

Virgil's happy shades in pure blanched raiment
Contend on their green meadows, while Orpheus
Weaves among them, sweeping strings, aswerve

To the pulse of his own playing and to avoid
The wrestlers, dancers, runners on the grass.
Not unlike a sports day in Bellaghy,

Slim Whitman's wavering tenor amplified
Above sparking dodgems, flying chair-o-planes,
A mile of road with parked cars in the twilight

And teams of grown men stripped for action
Going hell for leather until the final whistle,
Leaving stud-scrapes on the pitch and on each other.

xi

Those evenings when we'd just wait and watch
And fish. Then the evening the otter's head
Appeared in the flow, or was it only

A surface-ruck and gleam we took for
An otter's head? No doubting, all the same,
The gleam, a turnover warp in the black

Quick water. Or doubting the solid ground
Of the riverbank field, twilit and a-hover
With midge-drifts, as if we had commingled

Among shades and shadows stirring on the brink
And stood there waiting, watching,
Needy and ever needier for translation.

xii

And now the age of births. As when once
At dawn from the foot of our back garden
The last to leave came with fresh-plucked flowers

To quell whatever smells of drink and smoke
Would linger on where mother and child were due
Later that morning from the nursing home,

So now, as a thank-offering for one
Whose long wait on the shaded bank has ended,
I arrive with my bunch of stalks and silvered heads

Like tapers that won't dim
As her earthlight breaks and we gather round
Talking baby talk.

PHILIP MOSLEY *(translator)*

FRANÇOIS JACQMIN

The Book of the Snow

François Jacqmin's *The Book of the Snow* displays a poetry which is pure, abstract, and uncompromising, but also deeply felt, utterly precise, attuned to the complexity of the world. It takes the language of philosophy, of speculation and meditation, and adds to it a rich calm cadence; every image has a real and exact value. The short poems are surrounded with terms which seem to gesture towards saying something which is true and towards something else which is beyond mere truth. The central paradox of Jacqmin's poetry is the human mind's need to speak played against a profound suspicion of language. The unmarked snowy fields, the mind before thought, the blank silence that underlies all human expression — these are the slates on which these poems form and disintegrate. The poems in Philip Mosley's translation are thus filled with a mysterious beauty; they have a sort of shimmering quality. They are poems filled with both the world's weather and a weather which belongs to language purely and exquisitely shaped and sculpted.

—※—

Snow
overlays snow and cancels out its whiteness.
Everything lives and dies out
like that.
Being keeps house; at a stroke it
settles
the squall or the propensity to reason why.
Original certainty remains
thus,
by distinguishing nothing from nothing.

—※—

The time comes when hesitation reveals itself
as the most practical way of being in the world.
You watch the dissolution
of truth and matter
without emotion. Music is deemed slanderous
from the very first bars.
You no longer fuss over the absolute; you
consider it to be a
displaced melancholy,
an improper sadness.

When we follow the slope of an argument right down to
its proof,
we realize there is nothing to uphold.
Not knowing that the word
engenders more distance than does space,
some have resolved to speak as if starting
on their way
under a black northern sky. We found them
dead
in the white dust of meaning.

Gentlefolk stay at home.
Travel
reveals what is lamentable in the soul.
To go elsewhere is to
unstitch
the gather of innocence which innocence weaves
around our place.
It is the reason why I set great store on staying
at home amid my own things:
they are my common heartrending absolute.

—⁂—

For an inexhaustible instant, I sat down
by the snow.
My soul
which served as a refuge vanished and became
immensity
resting on immensity.
Perfection surged and abandoned all recourse
to reflection.
The snow
was within an inch of giving up as snow.

—⁂—

The cherries are packed tight in the belly
of the stones.
They sleep
in the scented constellation of a small almond
which yearns for
spring.
Their sleep is shameless.
They share the superb detachment of flowers
which will return and believe themselves
excused from death.

—⁂—

Frozen in its icy crypt, the fern is
intact,
but crushed by wintry non-decay.
Its eternity
is retained in a marble lock.
It attains
the highest degree of its concretion in a water
become
a bloc of parsimony.
It lies in its robust petrified dignity.

—⁂—

It is midnight.
The coal of the hour burns out in white
embers.
Remains of souls flicker
in the grate.
The shadows
hurl themselves at the walls like torn
birds of prey.
We remain alone,
with that fire which tries to rekindle itself.

—ϡ—

My ruin is not a work, nor
an oracle.
My self
is not a small town close to
the Pleiades.
I do not offer anyone the tribute of my
disaster. And I do not dedicate any of my poems.
For the soul,
it is enough to contemplate darkness which shows
darkness does not exist.

—ϡ—

I am delighted by this perpetual
impossible
which, in me, makes every project seem like
a taint.
I have enough fine arrogance to stay inactive for
a thousand years.
The night vainly pushes me toward literature.
Though my verse persists,
my poetics
is a merely honorary arrangement of words.

—◌—

The role
of the gaze is unknown if it is not to observe
that being
remains in the invisible
as water rushes over the rock without killing itself.
Being
wins out over the epic of the eye.
The object
you see is a prismatic nightmare,
a surveyor's downfall.

—◌—

Literary practice is an undistinguished
performance.
The lack
of finesse and the affront to decorum
appear with the very first word.
You who dispatch the snow with syntactical blows
show
your lack of breeding.
With you, whiteness is reduced to a common
style.

The tendency not to think is not an
aspect of night.
It is a practice
by which you reject
what arises in whatever dimension.
It is no longer a question of being according to
any way of being.
Thus you regain time which is neither time,
nor its wiping out,
nor even a winter's night under the snow.

We begin a verse like saying good evening
to a passer-by.
We strip him
furtively of his story.
We give him silent rebukes regarding
the time he has lost in not having been us.
Then we discover
that our monologue addresses
no one.
It is at this moment the poem's destiny begins.

He who had a single clear thought
may assert how strange was his life.
That sole light will make of him
one of those indeterminate beings who awaken
when you descend the slope
of sleep. He will be taken for someone who
does not aspire to any triumph or consent
to own any worldly goods.
He will be paralyzed by clarity,
and no one will wish to live with him.

Sometimes, in the night,
a bird sings without making itself heard.
At that moment,
thought obeys, that is to say, it
abstains. Then it becomes thought once more. It
reinstates the distraction of understanding
and of listening. It
abandons us to the oblivion of time
where we found ourselves
in that bird song unsung by the bird.

—∞—

The small scenes of childhood return
to memory.
The ambiguous warmth of family
evenings,
and the tiny incidents among the snowflakes
transform
their softness into childish
mysteries. You no longer divide
the allusions
to death from the joy of having been innocent.

—∞—

Moved
by an interior half-light, the observer,
sometimes, becomes attentive and
wary of observing.
Of this exemplary vision, he
retains but a pruned limb of the branches
of the visible.
Seeing nothing,
he embraces the flawless, leafless landscape.
He gazes upon the unmoved site of being.

—⁂—

The impossible is the unlimited sum of the poem.
It is the inaccessible nothing
which burns with a suppressed
fire
and which lights up the strange inability
to speak.
It shows off the insuperable and opens wide
what is overcome.
Endlessly it resoles the same thought
which lends itself to no traveller's foot.

—⁂—

With the snow
proclaiming that its essence
is a ceaseless distancing
from whiteness,
the word
aspires to be no longer expressible.
Everything clings to the axis of its own being
and speaks it while abstaining from doing so. It is thus
that I lose an arm
each time I write the word snow.

GJERTRUD SCHNACKENBERG

Heavenly Questions

Throughout her career, Gjertrud Schnackenberg has been widely admired for her elegant, inventive, and musically complex prosody, her emotional decorum, and her time-less frames of reference. *Heavenly Questions* is a book that has all of these qualities, yet moves far beyond them. Its six long poems tell a story of epic scale, creating a world large enough to contain Classical and Buddhist mythologies, a personal human drama of rare power, and the mathematics of physical existence (among many other things) while making them seem like entirely natural neighbours. This magic comes to us in a great upheaval of brilliant prosodic rule-breaking and reinvention. Describing these poems as blank verse heavily enriched by rhyme does not begin to describe the power of their formal realization. Reading this book is like reading the ocean, its swells and fur-rows, its secrets fleetingly revealed and then blown away in gusts of foam and spray or folded back into nothing but water. *Heavenly Questions* demands that we come face to face with matters of mortal importance, and it does so in a wildly original music that is passionate, transporting, and heart-rending.

Venus Velvet No. 2

My pencil, Venus Velvet No. 2,
The vein of graphite ore preoccupied
In microcrystalline eternity.
In graphite's interlinking lattices,
Symmetrically unfolding through a grid
Of pre-existent crystal hexagons.
Mirror-image planes and parallels.
Axial, infinitesimal bonds.
Self-generated. Self-geometrized.
A sound trapped in the graphite magnitudes.
Atoms, electrons, nuclei, far off.
A break, without apparent consequence.
Near-far, far-near, those microfirmaments.
Far in, the muffled noise of our goodbyes.

The surgeon, seeking only my surrender,
Has summoned me: an evening conference.
We sit together in the Quiet Room.
He cannot ask for what I'm meant to give.
No questions anymore. Just say he'll live.
A world of light leaks through the double doors,

Fluorescent mazes, frigid corridors,
Polished linoleum, arena sand
Where hope is put to death and life is lost
And elevator doors slide open, closed.
The towers of the teaching hospital.
The field where death *his conquering banner shook.*

My writing tablet, opened on the table.
I touch it with my hand. The paper thins.
The paper's interwoven filaments
Are bluish gray and beige. No questions now.
What is the chiefest deed that's asked of us.
No questions anymore. No questions now.
I turned my back on heaven for good, but saw
A banner shaken out from heaven's walls
With apparitions from Vesalius:
A woodcut surgeon opening a book
Of workshop woodcuts, skilled, anonymous,
The chisel blade of the engraver felt
Reverberating through the wooden blocks
Among eroded words, ornately carved:
Annihilation, subtly engraved:
All those whom lamentation cannot save
Grown fainter through successive folios.
A seraph turns a page above: he'll live;
Then turns a page again: he can't survive.
I turn the page myself, and write: he'll live.
Smell of my sweat embedded in my clothes.

The surgeon says: we've talked with him; he knows.
A seraph leaning near, *Oh say not so.*
Not so. Not so. My wonder-wounded hearer,
Facing extinction in a mental mirror.
A brilliant ceiling, someone's hand on his.
All labor, effort, sacrifice, recede.
And then: I'm sorry. Such a man he is.

Visionary crystallography.
Electron noise brimming in pencil lead.
A sound trapped in the graphite magnitudes.
Far in, the muffled noise of our goodbyes
In self-repeating crystal symmetries
As graphite self-destructs in shearing off
Abraded words and microcrystals break
In microscopic heaps of graphite dust:
My pencil, scribbling, giving up on us:

A pinpoint leak of blood that can't be traced.
A mass embedded underneath the heart.
Hepatic portal vein that routes the blood
Throughout the tract of the intestine maze
And soaks the liver's capillary beds.
The intima. A bleeding deep inside.
Something smaller than a grain of sand.
Mechanisms poorly understood.
All that could be done has now been done.
I write the words, with vitals liquefied.

A page is turned above: it did no good.
A page is turned again: it did no good.
Then fingers touch a page that can't be turned.

But if it did no good, then how could I
Have watched as toxins dripped how many times
Into his bluest veins from hanging tubes
With hypodermic fangs, and how could he
Have offered up his veins without a word,
Except to reassure me it's all right
And never lose his confidence and wait
Throughout how many closed eternities,
Like Theseus bound to a chair with snakes.
The ship of Theseus passing overhead.
Our hands entwined: a single heart drained white.
And all that could be done has now been done
And I sat by. Seat of oblivion.
And saw, behind the hypodermic fangs,
The long pink throats of snakes, and sat chairbound,
And spellbound, and heartbound, and cobra-struck,
Though for his sake I would have risen up
To crush the jaws of snakes with my bare hands.

The tablet paper, thinning at my touch.
— He said of you, Nothing can conquer her. —
The words appear, the pencil unaware
Of what it writes: *But you did know how much*,
Words of defeated Antony, when all
Was lost, in graphite's faded gray: *But you*
Did know how much you were my conqueror.

The tablet paper, bluish gray and beige.
The graphite pressed and bound with binding clay.
Graphite, a non-magnetic mineral.
Yet magnets hold the phrases to the page.

A brilliant ceiling light, the god's blue glove,
The gesture at the opened body's rim:
All that could be done has now been done.
One and the Many. Many and the One.

How could I turn and say: but this is him.
How could I say: he bounded when he walked.
How could I say: when he came home at night,
A gust of snowy air around his coat,
I drew him closer, holding his lapels;
He caught me by the wrists and closed his eyes.

How could I say I tried to memorize
The truthful face, his smile a truthful blaze
Untrammeled still. I tried to learn by heart
The light-brown gaze: unguarded chrysolite
From such another world that heaven made.
Left iris, with a comet-fleck of gold.
How could I memorize his gentle ways.
The way he mingled friendliness with passion,
Plain dealing, open-handed, unafraid.
The swift, reflexive generosity.

His striking conversation, magic ease
In seeking what the other could, then more,
In understanding, warmly understood;
A quest for truth but not for certainty.

And the integrity I idolized:
Another's mystery never trifled with.
No one was belittled in those eyes.

Nothing denied, held back, or kept apart.
And never lost his gentle ways with me.
And wanted power over no one else,
But master of his heart, and of himself,
A mind that never darkened, mastermind,
Fountain of pulsing energy at play,
Unshackled, unentangled, unconfined.

Beneath the reading light, his pillowed head
A crimson-outlined silhouette at night,
His profile marble-carved, noble, sun-warmed,
Even at night, in winter, ruddy-tinged.
Red-gold of Titian's pigment-laden brush.

The red-lit aureate curving of his ear,
Warm-blooded velvet, made for lips to find.
I kissed his brow good night and felt the touch
Of lashes brush my chin before they closed.
Untroubled love. Unmarred. And quiet sleep,

His head a silken weight against my chest,
Velvet inner elbow, dangled foot,
Voluptuous surrender, unarmed Mars,
Even in sleep, composed. Even in sleep
Possessive of my hand. Still self-possessed.

Never again our idyll-nights of peace,
Never again to have him to myself.
White sheets, white blanket shadows, whitest rest,

His sleeping hand beneath the reading light
Abandoning an ancient paperback
Of Buddhist parables that fell away
When I retrieved it, dropping page by page:

Oh say not so, Ananda, say not so,
Buddha replied, when his pupil-companion
Came to him, and sat down on one side,
And set aside his begging bowl, and said,
"My teacher, isn't beauty half the goal?
For doesn't half the holy life consist
Of drawing near to beauty, step by step?"
Oh say not so, Ananda, say not so;
Not half, he answered. *Say it is the whole.*

My pencil point, hallucinating scrolls,
Scrolling and unscrolling on the page.
A wind was pushing shapes through waves of water,
But whether shapes of water or of wind,

Impossible to say: unscrolling waves
In slow velocities and solitudes

Unwheeling in volutes and streaming spheres
And transitory sets of spiral stairs
That climb-descend themselves, and disappear
On wheeling waterwheels in waterwheels,
Expending wave-momentum piling up

Black waves in heaps, then turning oceans white;
Black troughs, white crests, black troughs, directionless
But pulling back, then pushing east to west
And west to east, black troughs, directionless,
Endings accumulating endlessly
And gathering accumulated force
How many thousand miles, and all to press

Ahead, but to what end, all for the sake
Of using oceanic force to lay
A fringe of foam along a passing crest,
Then pulling foam down transitory walls
And pushing walls ahead, and all to break
In momentary peaks along a shore
We can't say where, and briefly taking back
What's briefly given, everything in play,
In gulfs that close and open; close again;

And waves of water pushing shapes through wind,
And each the other's mine, no gulfs to cross
But crossing gulfs in turn, and historyless —

How could I say we wanted nothing else
And nothing less and nothing more than this,
To find each other's spirit's melting point
And changing states, never such nakedness
Between such two, *my bluest veins to kiss*,
Never such certainty, the selfsame quest

Not to possess, but to be known; to know;
Not needing it confirmed; confirming it.
And in a place arrived at on our knees,
He tugged my face to his, as if he took
His own life in his hands; all gentle ways;
A lifelong quest for you; and won't let go
Unless you leave your fingerprints on me;
A gaze returned, the softest counterblow;

And gathering my hair in gentle fists,
Persuasion's force with no one to persuade,
Only persuading hairpins from my hair,
Their falling on the floor, a plunder-gift;

And nothing lost, but found and found again;
And not conquest, but everything in play
Given, not taken; taken anyway,
And not to keep in any case; but kept;
Possessed, but not in order to possess;
Selfsame, self-owned, self-given, self-possessed,
And all in play. But conquered nonetheless.

The yellow maze of frigid corridors
Shone black; it didn't matter where; I left,
But sightless, pulling on my winter coat,
My boots pulled over sweatpants, hat and gloves
Pulled on, indoors; as if to take him home;

A maze of concrete blocks, and doors in rows
In halls and hallways swallowing the rooms
And blind corners that swallowed up the halls
And elevator doors slid open, closed
On hollow towers built in the negative
Where bells, plunged from their ropes, were falling past.
A crust of unshed tears above my throat.
Give him back. Tell me what I can give.
Without an altar, death. Without a place
To pray. To beg for life. But let him live.

I found a phone booth, place to bawl unheard,
And sank beneath its automatic light.
The phone book hanging from a broken chain —
I drew it to my lap, a sprawling weight
Of paper pulp from long-forgotten trees
Snuffed-out and boiled down and pressed in sheets
Of ashen paper, faintly blue and gray,
A book unreadable and authorless,
A mystical directory of the living,
Each page a random sample of Creation
And changing version of the Book of Life;
I ran my glove over the listings: throngs;

And found his name, still listed with the living,
Whose stories vanish, leaving only names
Recycled and reused. This faring on
And on, O mendicants. And overhead

A page that can't be turned. He can't survive.
But let him live. My gloves pressing my eyes,
A thousand stars rotating inwardly
A millimeter past the streamered dark,
And nameless comet-phosphenes streaking by.
Without an altar, death. Without a place.

Hanging in mirror-black, lit from above,
My frightened face, kneaded in violet wax.
My face, hanging above my lap, streamed out.
I tried to press it back with clumsy gloves.

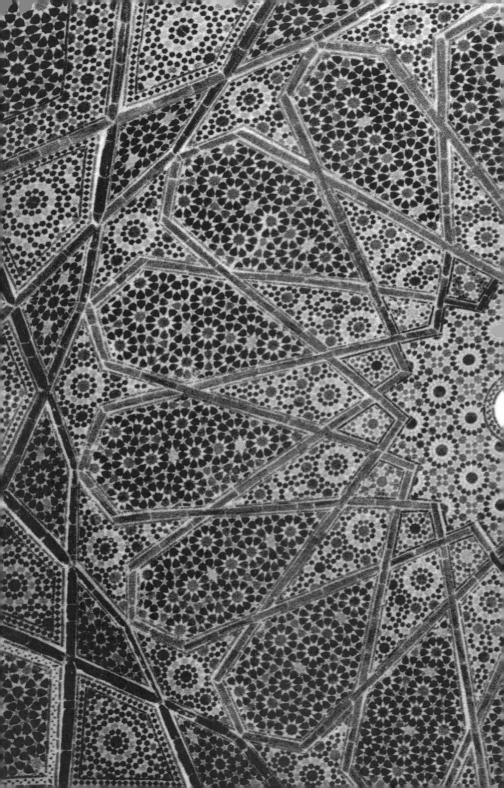

CANADIAN
FINALISTS

DIONNE BRAND

Ossuaries

What Dionne Brand has done in *Ossuaries* is amazing. Working with a novel-length narrative about the life of an activist named Yasmine, who lives an underground existence on various continents, she has constructed a long poem, which is not a traditional seamless epic, nor a Poundian extended collage, but something else that seems quite new. The most remarkable part of her achievement is that in fulfilling the novelistic narrative ambition of her work, she has not sacrificed the tight lyrical coil of the poetic line. The story vaults us ahead with its emerging and receding characters, its passions and dramas, which include a violent bank robbery and tense escape, while each line holds us and demands we admire its complex beauties. The sensation of hurtling and, at the same time, being caught is uncanny. Brand's innovation in *Ossuaries* calls forth an entirely new sort of reading. The book is a triumph.

ossuary II

to undo, to undo and undo and undo this infinitive
of arrears, their fissile mornings,
their fragile, fragile symmetries of gain and loss

this is how she wakes each day of each underground year,
confessions late and half-hearted pour from her sleeping
mouth, beginning in the year of her disappearances

the grateful rooms had to be gathered into their temporal
shapes, the atmosphere coaxed to visible
molecules, definite arrangements of walls and doors

solidity lies beside her in its stigmatic shreds,
I, the slippery pronoun, the ambivalent, glistening,
long sheath of the alphabet flares beyond her reach

how then to verify her body, rejuvenate the blood-dead
arm, quell her treacherous stomach, its heaving solar
jumps, or seduce the preposition, where and where

her neck crackles to the radio voice, that coastal beacon,
last night she exchanged one set of keys for another,
her palms, branched, copper basins outstretched

now one numb finger, one thumb searched,
through all their known grammars for which
room, which dewy bed, and then what fateful day

nearsighted she needs her glasses yes, to summarize
the world, without them she's defenceless,
that's why they're always at the precipice of the bed

some violent drama was as usual surging,
on the airwaves and "plane" she heard, the usual
supercilious timbres hysterical, a cut larynx

she thought of splinters, slivering boards,
scooped the glasses from her abdomen to align
her brain, here notice, notice what is false from true

what is possible, and where's the doorway of this room,
kinetic news breaking sunlight,
but where was she, which city, what street

Albany, Buffalo, Havana, back tracks, Algiers,
to the swift boat ride from the south of Spain, back when,
the brief embossed room, a reversal, a body at sea

then, the short wave asserted, Manhattan,
Yasmine's tingling hand summoned the volume
in its circumference of black plastic, she

could not be in Manhattan, though the radio insisted,
her back alert like paintings to its usual ache,
some mornings she could return to sleep even

in the middle of the most gruesome news,
caught,
caught, every comrade caught

she could delay events with this groggy chemistry
of spasms and refusals,
a drowning, that second sleep, in lists of the undone

ungiven, unsought, the nausea could last days,
this room took shape now in yellow and brown,
a window lay behind a wilting curtain, tepid sunlight

the radio veered once again toward her, speeding,
"explosion," it mourned,
a kitchen knife, spanner, tweezers, skill saw

she felt a joy innocent like butter open her,
blinding stratus, ants, tongs, bolts, rust,
the whole ionosphere bounced into her mouth

glancing against her teeth, exceeding her nostrils, her
heart burrowed,
in corks, broken bottles, nails, finned incendiaries

she flew like shrapnel off the bed,
felt her way blind, as fire with slender strands,
as glaze, sand, starch caps, uniforms, and bracelets

the prepositions are irrelevant today, whichever house,
which century, wherever she was,
the bruised wires, severed, this they only ever dreamed

she would love, love to talk to them today,
though the dreaming had come to little and no end,
and less, there in the grey blood of the television

the spectacular buildings falling limpid, to nothing,
rims, aluminum, windowless, fragile staircases,
she wanted, wanted to whisper into telephones

it's done, someone had done it, someone,
had made up for all the failures,
she looked, pitiless, at the rubble, the shocked

the stumbling shattered dressed for work,
the powdering towers, the walls and windows
stuck to their skins like makeup and grease

look, the seared handbags, the cooked briefcases,
wheels, clocks, the staggered floors,
the startled one-winged orioles

the flights of starlings interrupted,
the genocides of September insects,
the disappearances after of sugar bees and quick footsteps

it was just past nine in any city,
but a glass of wine would do, a beer, a toke,
here's to the fatal future

how many times they'd asked each other,
you are ready to die but are you ready to kill,
she had been willing once

a jealousy orbiting her skull, its brittle calcium,
outside everywhere burned skin,
would she have flown into that willing skin

what equations she wondered of steel's pressure,
and concrete, matter and vacuum and terrible faith,
of sacred books, of tattooed foreheads, of small knives

she believed in nothing too, not broken hearts,
not blood with wine, not beloveds,
not the weight of her eyelids nor her own intentions

not even people whom she'd once admitted
were her hopes, and what she'd calculated
all her acts against

but failure is when they describe what you've done,
and she lives in that description hand to mouth,
outside the everyday, in refugee shafts

and tiny rooms, and in other people's passports,
in mathematical theorems of trust,
in her vigilant skin and feathery, feathery deceit

it is not enough to change the bourgeois state,
this sentence slumbered in her, sleek,
you have to bring it down, winched to this

each dawn's lurid ambivalence,
the chest fire flaring on any sofa, any chair, any bed,
the calculus of infidelity on each forehead kissed

she read the periodic table of elements in an eyebrow,
the length of patience in love,
this moment to depart in coffee's taste

fall crept now in the rind of deciduous stems,
and she could read it seconds before it arrived,
and hear birds and their music head south like musicians

packing up kit, decamping stale beer-smelling
halls, the floors' sly self-serving penitence,
the dismissive flutter of high-speed wings

it was sunny, a pale sunny, and the lindens down
three storeys spun their leaves tipped yellow,
grim joy overtook her

come the true fall here, come the fall, the romance
with the air is over but now,
now, who has such mortal imagination

her joy was not grim, her knuckles knotted in her lap,
insisted, yes she is aware that joy is grim, how these
two make a marriage, how long their courtship in her

house finches in the eavestroughs
went about their fall business, remorseless,
their urban quickness, their rapid knowledgeable song

and she had mourned enough for a thousand
broken towers, her eyesight washed immaculate and
caustic, her whole existence was mourning, so what?

SUZANNE BUFFAM

The Irrationalist

Suzanne Buffam's *The Irrationalist* takes nothing for granted. Its rhythms manage to mimic the mind at work, the mind edgy and witty and sharp. The tones are brave and sweeping, ready to re-define the world, alert not only to history and the exigencies of the contemporary, but also to larger questions to do with philosophy, with time and space. Buffam's talent is to find the startling, telling phrase, arranging and turning her lines and cadences with considerable surprise and flair. Some of the poems are funny; others capture culture and nature, or the connections between them, with intelligence, originality, and wisdom. Her poetic systems are bathed in irony, but she is also capable of allowing language to soar. In her three-line poem "On Last Lines," she sums up the power of her own poetic gift: "The last line should strike like a lover's complaint. / You should never see it coming. / And you should never hear the end of it."

Ruined Interior

In the beginning was the world.
Then the new world.
Then the new world order

Which resembles the old one,
Doesn't it? Its crumbling
Aqueducts. Its trinkets and shingles.

Its pathways lacquered in fog.
If all we've done is blink a bit
And touch things,

Notice how dust describes
A tin can by not falling
Where it sits, or how a red sleeve

Glimpsed through curtains
Mimics the tip of a flickering
Wing, was the whole day a waste

Or can worth be conferred
On a less than epic urge? Bow-wow
Says the doggie on page two.

Ahoy says the sailor.
Arise says the tired queen
And face the highway

The donut shops, and the boardwalk.
It rained today. You can see
Perfect inversions of streetlights

Suspended in drops on the window.
You can see the skyline
Trying to hold up the sky.

Don't tell me there's another,
Better place. Don't tell me
There's a sea

Above our dreaming sea
And through the windows of heaven
The rains come down.

The New Experience

I was ready for a new experience.
All the old ones had burned out.

They lay in little ashy heaps along the roadside
And blew in drifts across the fairgrounds and fields.

From a distance some appeared to be smouldering
But when I approached with my hat in my hands

They let out small puffs of smoke and expired.
Through the windows of houses I saw lives lit up

With the otherworldly glow of TV
And these were smoking a little bit too.

I flew to Rome. I flew to Greece.
I sat on a rock in the shade of the Acropolis

And conjured dusky columns in the clouds.
I watched waves lap the crumbling coast.

I heard wind strip the woods.
I saw the last living snow leopard

Pacing in the dirt. Experience taught me
That nothing worth doing is worth doing

For the sake of experience alone.
I bit into an apple that tasted sweetly of time.

The sun came out. It was the old sun
With only a few billion years left to shine.

from **Little Commentaries**

On Quandariness

I do not know which to prefer
The beauty of Nova Scotia
Or the beauty of France.
Ducks landing on the saltmarsh
Or poached in their fat on my plate.

On Flags

Few things are more stirring
Than a flag in the wind.
A problem of aesthetics vs. ethics.
All morning I study
A tea towel drying on the line.
A flag without a country
Is like desire without an end.

On Joy

Joy unmixed with sorrow
Is like a fountain turned off at night.

On Clear Nights

At most two thousand stars
Can be seen with the naked eye from earth.

A difficult number to grapple with.
Too large, and, on the other hand, too small.

A simple mathematical equation
May throw the problem into relief.

Consider a battlefield.
The fighting has ended

And the bodies lie still in the grass.
How many dead soldiers

Equal the sky overhead?

Dim-Lit Interior

I'm done crying in my beer about love.

My days of riding the shiny brass school bus are behind me as well.

The changes come slowly but suddenly.

One day the sun will burn so brightly it will turn all our seas into vast boiling vats.

Freedom comes from understanding our inability to change things.

So lead me O Destiny whither is ordained by your decree.

Just please don't force me to vacuum the stairs.

The quiet that follows the storm may be the same as the quiet before it.

Let the wind blow.

Let it blow down each tree on the bright boulevard.

The things I would most like to change are the things that make me believe change is possible.

JOHN STEFFLER

Lookout

The playful spontaneity that enlivens John Steffler's *Lookout*
moves through the poems like wind, revealing both their
flexibility and their sturdiness. With a passionate natural-
ist's trained and ever-curious eye, Steffler is interested in
what happens both in and out of sight.

In language that ranges from affable story-telling to
tough, spare, startling lyrics, he probes the complex
collisions between Nature and humankind without inflict-
ing upon his subject any of the ecological ranting, self-
dramatizing grief, or faux-mysticism that infects so much
contemporary "nature poetry." Modest, plainspoken, and
unsentimental in stance, his poems are at the same time
untethered to the literal, which allows for sudden and
unnerving swerves, poems that decisively and unpredict-
ably break the membrane between realms, as when a vole
with "a laugh like a snowplow's blade" begins to speak, or
rifts appear in a loved one's memory, allowing reality and
fantasy, past and present, to dissolve into one another.
Steffler's quality of attention is so fierce and so assured that
we trust it to lead us into new and often unsettling territory.
In *Lookout*, his masterful inter-leaving of physical, philo-
sophical, and psychological worlds entices us into a dream
of wakefulness we recognize as our own.

Cape Norman

Past the last house the gravel track widens to the horizon,

and seeing better and better,
you negotiate the innumerable stones'
deepening textures — the wheel ruts' buttes and wadis
leading the eye down a long maze — until stopped
by the lighthouse,

                              sea's plunge and assault,
gannet-owned — the beacon's rolling blink,
the giant repeated groan a conceptual monument
declaring our nation's response to the place:
a seizure
mechanically enacted for us all.

At the mist-blown cliff you scramble down tumbled blocks
once bone —
                    prehuman Egypt,
gods' jaws, twenty-ton lintels, upended stairs.

Blue shell ceramic flakes in thin drifts, salt-jewellery
fragments sharp on the palms.

In a crevice, a tuft of white grass-hairs, bobbing —
pocked foreheads, worm script on the gods' grey chins.

Daily for five hundred million years *The Paleozoic Times*
was delivered here — vast page laid upon page, accidents,

killings, jackpots, plagues, fused and fractured — you
crawl on the lost familiar text,
nylon hood flapping your ear.

Wind Shadow, L'Anse aux Meadows

Wind off the Strait of Belle Isle rakes
the cape clean. Anything wanting to live here
finds it enjoys crouching in a still pocket
behind a rock (eight months of the year
a white drift) where once in a while a companion
will tumble in: an ant's leg or cinquefoil leaf.
Just arrived is a scuffed mountain avens seed,
which in the next rain might burst its seams and
help pack the small summer room with green, except
for the week in July when it will parody snow.

Leif Eriksson dropped the erratic fact
of his briefly inhabited outpost here,
and now the fascination of tourists gusts
over the ancient site, their exclamations
and money tumble into the shadow it casts
along Route 436, feeding a clump
of restaurants, gift shops, B&Bs, new
bright-painted homes. The local people want
more boulders like L'Anse aux Meadows, more
nooks where money drifts in, especially now
that the Strait is raked clean of cod.

Notes on Burnt Cape

Frost causes rock to boil — wedging ice into cracks, it
splits stones, then slips its water blades deeper in,
levers them, spades the gravel up in rolling domes.

On the scraped-bare cape each strewn boulder has a wind
shadow (pointing southeast) — a tapered green plant-woven
satchel stuffed with silt.

Trees, spilt like puzzle pieces, grow their branches
down among stones as though into air, and you
must lie down to distinguish the crowns of the willows
and birch.

Sky and sea vault away beyond reckoning — your car,
the road you followed, your house, you have to work
to recall.

Sometimes caught in the wind's cold pelt, pure
sounds — waves' leisurely slosh or thump, gulls'
high slow staccato — brush past the ear
like ocean's barbed seeds.

Beyond Names and Laws

On Jackson Island Jim snared a rabbit,
skinned it, and worked a half-pound hook
up through its bare muscled ass, its rib cage
and throat, until the barbed tip lodged
in back of its eyes, then tied the hook to a line
as thick as Huck's thumb and let it trail
in the river's pull all night from their raft
moored among willow boughs,
                              and in the morning
hauled what he first took for a sunk stump,
its streaming roots the snaky beard of the biggest
catfish they'd ever seen. It was dead on the line.
They couldn't lift it. They would have towed the monster
to town and sold it and been talked about for years,
if they hadn't been on the run. Made one white
notch in its mossy back, enough for their morning
meal, then cut the line to let the dark
thing roll on ahead of them.

Mail from My Pregnant Daughter

An envelope with your rounded printing. I take out
a card of Henri Rousseau's *Child with Doll* —
the stocky worried girl in a red dress, clutching
a worried doll, listening, knowing the whole
landscape is going to erupt through her, life
will depend on her —

                    then your twelve-week
ultrasound with its five night-blue images
framed in calibrations and ID.
I have albums tracing your quick expressions back
to your infancy, but here I'm looking at moonlight
falling into an excavated grave. Or is it
a distant galaxy? The small gathering bones
glow where faint light picks them out,
a constellation of vertebrae. Hubble
portrait. Reverse grave.

                  What a woman holds —
river of earth from the Milky Way, where we hatch,
to which we return. From my unwinding whorl I'm looking
through your night sky at forming stars.
Inside those I can almost see smaller stars.

from **Once**

—▱—

The neighbour's lawn mower roars and recedes.
My mother sleeps on the loveseat, my father
on the couch. I shake out mats on the blinding
porch, gather grey tea towels for the laundry.
My father bustles stiffly out to plug in
the kettle, comes up from the cellar with chunks
of maple, measuring, figuring — how to make
wooden nuts and bolts — then is suddenly
sunk in an armchair, open-mouthed asleep,
while June sunlight storms through the house.

—ᴍ—

I ask about the empty mirror frame on the kitchen
wall. My father glances at me and away, looking
reluctant, caught. Then speaks with odd formality,
doggedly, against some current of shyness or disbelief
or sorrow or fear. He says while they were having
lunch there at the table a few weeks ago they heard
a loud bang like a gunshot close by. He looked around
and found the mirror down on the floor, its heavy glass
split up the middle. "*You* try to get that off of there,"
he points to the empty frame. A slotted hole in its back
locks the frame tight to a round-headed screw set deep
in a wall stud. I lift and slowly work it free, then press it
back into place, centred, anchored. Enclosed blank
wall. "There's no way that could have come off
by itself," he says, bare-headed under low dark cloud.

Curled on the loveseat under a blanket
much of each day, sleeping or merely
still, her open eyes travelling the room.

She never grieves for herself, never
stands apart disowning or lamenting
the ruin, but sometimes terrors sweep
through her, weightless spinning and inner
sleets, and she sits shaking, calling out that
she's falling, and my father or I hold her
trying to save her from deep space.

Blomidon Head

In the evening, in every season and weather, Mount
Blomidon's bronze head floats over the valley
and Arm, smiling a smile that is not one
we understand — more a pleased stasis that looks
to us like a smile because in spite of cold or heat
or cloud or helicopters or prospectors' stakes or
funeral processions along Route 406 it never
changes. It looms serene black-purple, black-green
in the dark, and the houses ring its base like flickering
candles. But once when I was in its presence alone
it played a tiny piano and looked sideways at me
uncertainly to see if I enjoyed the tune. And
another time it said in a small girl's voice, "The wind
kept me awake all night. Hold my feet, please, squeeze
them hard, and my ankles." And a vole I had glimpsed
scuttling under the blueberry leaves then startled me
with a laugh that was like a snowplow's blade
shaking the road, "I have eaten cities in Azerbaijan
and Peru, you will never find their foundations,
I have crossed glaciers and slept through fires
that left nothing but black nutshells and bones."

ABOUT THE POETS

ADONIS (born Ali Ahmad Said Esber) is a Syrian poet and essayist who led the modernist movement in Arabic poetry in the second half of the twentieth century. He has written more than twenty books in his native Arabic, including the pioneering work *An Introduction to Arab Poetics*. Adonis received the Bjørnston Prize in 2007, the first International Nâzim Hikmet Poetry Award, the Syria-Lebanon Best Poet Award, and the highest award of the International Poem Biennial in Brussels. Elected a member of the Stéphane Mallarmé Academy in 1983, he lives in Paris.

DIONNE BRAND's previous collections of poetry include *Land to Light On*, winner of the Governor General's Literary Award for Poetry and the Trillium Book Award; *thirsty*, winner of the Pat Lowther Memorial Award and a finalist for the Trillium Book Award, the Toronto Book Award, and the Griffin Poetry Prize; and *Inventory*, a finalist for the Pat Lowther Memorial Award and the Governor General's Literary Award for Poetry. In 2006, Brand was awarded the prestigious Harbourfront Festival Prize, and in 2009, she was named Toronto's Poet Laureate.

SUZANNE BUFFAM's first collection of poetry, *Past Imperfect*, won the Gerald Lampert Memorial Award for Poetry and was named a *Globe and Mail* "Top 100" Book of the Year. She won the 1998 CBC Literary Award for Poetry and has twice been shortlisted for a Pushcart Prize. Born and raised in Canada, she currently teaches Creative Writing at the University of Chicago.

SEAMUS HEANEY was born in Northern Ireland. *Death of a Naturalist*, his first collection, appeared in 1966, and since then he has published poetry, criticism, and translations that have established him as one of the leading poets of his generation. He has twice won the Whitbread Book of the Year award, for *The Spirit Level* and *Beowulf*. In 1995 he was awarded the Nobel Prize in Literature. *District and Circle*, his eleventh collection of poems, was published in 2006 and was awarded the T. S. Eliot Prize.

FRANÇOIS JACQMIN, acknowledged as one of the foremost francophone Belgian poets of the latter half of the twentieth century, was born in 1929 in Horion-Hozémont in the province of Liège. In 1940 his family fled to England to escape the German occupation. He returned to Belgium in 1948 and rediscovered his native language and literature. His three major volumes of poetry are *Les Saisons*, *Le Domino gris*, and *Le Livre de la neige*. *Eléments de géométrie*, a volume of prose poems written a few years before his death in 1992, was published in 2005.

KHALED MATTAWA is associate professor of English language and literature at the University of Michigan. Born in Benghazi, Libya, he emigrated to the United States as a teenager. He is the author of four books of poetry, most recently *Tocqueville*, and has translated five books of Arab poetry. Mattawa has received a PEN award for literary translation, a Guggenheim Fellowship, and two Pushcart Prizes. He has recently been selected by the Academy of American Poets as the recipient of the 2010 Academy Fellowship.

PHILIP MOSLEY is Professor of English and Comparative Literature at Pennsylvania State University. He earned his M.A. in European literature and his Ph.D. in comparative literature from the University of East Anglia. He has translated *The Intelligence of Flowers* by Maurice Maeterlinck, *Bruges-la-Morte* by Georges Rodenbach, *Tea Masters, Teahouses* by Werner Lambersy, and *October Long Sunday* by Guy Vaes. In 2008 he was awarded the Prix de la Traduction Littéraire by the French Community of Belgium for his translations of Belgian authors into English.

GJERTRUD SCHNACKENBERG was born in Tacoma, Washington, in 1953. She is the author of five collections of poetry, including *The Throne of Labdacus*, which won the 2001 *Los Angeles Times* Book Prize in Poetry and was named a *New York Times* Book Review Notable Book of 2000. She received the Lavan Younger Poets Award (judged by Robert Fitzgerald) from the Academy of American Poets, and the Rome Prize in Literature from the American Academy and Institute of Arts and Letters.

JOHN STEFFLER was the Parliamentary Poet Laureate of Canada from 2006 to 2008. His previous books of poetry include *The Grey Islands*, *That Night We Were Ravenous*, winner of the Atlantic Poetry Prize, and *Helix: New and Selected Poems*, winner of the Newfoundland and Labrador Poetry Prize. Steffler is also the author of the award-winning novel *The Afterlife of George Cartwright*.

ABOUT THE JUDGES

TIM LILBURN was born in Regina, Saskatchewan. He has published eight books of poetry, including *To the River, Kill-site*, and *Orphic Politics*. He has received the Governor General's Literary Award for Poetry (for *Kill-site*) and the Saskatchewan Book of the Year Award (for *To the River*), among other prizes. Lilburn has written two essay collections, both concerned with poetics, eros, and politics: *Living in the World as if It Were Home* and *Going Home*. In addition, he has edited two collections on poetics, *Poetry and Knowing* and *Thinking and Singing: Poetry and the Practice of Philosophy*. He was a participant in the 2008 Pamirs Poetry Journey. Lilburn teaches at the University of Victoria.

COLM TÓIBÍN is the author of six novels, including *The Master*, winner of the International IMPAC Dublin Literary Award and shortlisted for the Man Booker Prize, and named the *Los Angeles Times* Novel of the Year and the Meilleur Livre Étranger in France, and *Brooklyn*, winner of the Costa Prize for Novel of the Year in the UK. He has been a visiting writer at Stanford University and the University of Texas at Austin. He is currently Leonard Milberg Lecturer in Irish Letters at Princeton. He is a regular contributor to the *London Review of Books* and the *New York Review of Books*. His work has been translated into thirty languages.

CHASE TWICHELL has published seven books of poetry: *Horses Where the Answers Should Have Been: New & Selected Poems, Dog Language, The Snow Watcher, The Ghost of Eden, Perdido, The Odds*, and *Northern Spy*. She is also the translator, with Tony K. Stewart, of *The Lover of God* by Rabindranath Tagore, and co-editor of *The Practice of Poetry: Writing Exercises from Poets Who Teach*. She has received fellowships from the National Endowment for the Arts, the Artists Foundation, the New Jersey State Council on the Arts, and the John Simon Guggenheim Memorial Foundation, as well as a Literature Award from the American Academy of Arts and Letters. In 2010 Twichell was awarded an honorary doctorate from St. Lawrence University. A student in the Mountains and Rivers Order at Zen Mountain Monastery, she lives in upstate New York with her husband, the novelist Russell Banks.

ACKNOWLEDGEMENTS

The publisher thanks the following for their kind permission to reprint the work contained in this volume:

"Psalm," "Not a Star," "Flower of Alchemy," "Man's Song," "Woman's Song," and "I Imagine a Poet" from *Selected Poems* by Adonis, translated by Khaled Mattawa, are reprinted by permission of Yale University Press.

"ossuary II" from *Ossuaries* by Dionne Brand is reprinted by permission of McClelland & Stewart.

"Route 110" from *Human Chain* by Seamus Heaney is reprinted by permission of Farrar, Straus and Giroux.

The selections from *The Book of the Snow* by François Jacqmin, translated by Philip Mosley, are reprinted by permission of Arc Publications.

"Venus Velvet No. 2" from *Heavenly Questions* by Gjertrud Schnackenberg is reprinted by permission of Farrar, Straus and Giroux.

"Cape Norman," "Wind Shadow, L'Anse aux Meadows," "Notes on Burnt Cape," "Beyond Names and Laws," "Mail from My Pregnant Daughter," selections from "Once," and "Blomidon Head" from *Lookout* by John Steffler are reprinted by permission of McClelland & Stewart.

THE 2011 GRIFFIN POETRY
PRIZE ANTHOLOGY

Books of poetry published in English internationally and in Canada are honoured each year with the $65,000 Griffin Poetry Prize, one of the world's most prestigious and valuable literary awards. Since 2001 this annual prize has acted as a tremendous spur to interest in and recognition of poetry, focusing worldwide attention on the formidable talent of poets writing in English. Each year the editor of *The Griffin Poetry Prize Anthology* compiles the work of the extraordinary poets shortlisted for the awards and introduces us to some of the finest poems in their collections.

This year, editor and prize juror Tim Lilburn's selections from the international shortlist include poems from Adonis's *Selected Poems* (Yale University Press), translated by Khaled Mattawa, Seamus Heaney's *Human Chain* (Farrar, Straus and Giroux), François Jacqmin's *The Book of the Snow* (Arc Publications), translated by Philip Mosley, and Gjertrud Schnackenberg's *Heavenly Questions* (Farrar, Straus and Giroux). The selection from the Canadian shortlist includes poems from Dionne Brand's *Ossuaries* (McClelland & Stewart), Suzanne Buffam's *The Irrationalist* (House of Anansi Press), and John Steffler's *Lookout* (McClelland & Stewart).

In choosing the 2011 shortlist, prize jurors Tim Lilburn, Colm Tóibín, and Chase Twichell considered 450 collections published in the previous year, including 20 translations from poets in 37 countries. The jury also wrote the citations that introduce the seven poets' nominated works.

Royalties generated from *The 2011 Griffin Poetry Prize Anthology* will be donated to UNESCO's World Poetry Day, which was created to support linguistic diversity through poetic expression and to offer endangered languages the opportunity to be heard in their communities.